T0121826

POETIC EXPRESSIONS
for
TRAVELERS

L. Alex Swan

Order this book online at www.trafford.com
or email orders@trafford.com

Most Trafford titles are also available at major online book retailers.

Printed in the United States of America.

ISBN: 978-1-4669-8473-8 (sc)
ISBN: 978-1-4669-8476-9 (e)

Trafford rev. 03/07/2013

 www.trafford.com

North America & international
toll-free: 1 888 232 4444 (USA & Canada)
phone: 250 383 6864 ♦ fax: 812 355 4082

CONTENTS

THE TREE OF KNOWLEDGE

THE BIBLE CONTAINS 3,566,480 letters, 773,693 words, 31,102 verses, 1,189 chapters and 66 books. The longest chapter is the 119th Psalm, the shortest and middle chapter is the 117th psalm. The middle verse is the 8th of the 118th Psalm. The longest name is in the 8th chapter of isaiah. The word occurs 46,277 times, the word "Jehovah" occurs 6,855 times. The 37th chapter of Isaiah and the 19th chapter of the 2nd book of Kings are alike. The longest verse is the 9th verse of the 8th chapter of Esther; the shortest verse is the 35th of the 11th chapter of John. The 21st verse of the 7th chapter of Ezra contains all the letters of the alphabet except the letter "J". The finest piece of reading is the 26th chapter of Acts. The name of God is not mentioned in the book of Esther. The bible contains knowledge, wisdom, holiness, and love.

FOREWORD

THE POEMS IN THIS work were written at various times, places and during various events in the life of the author. They all represent his reflection at the moment of inspiration. None of the poems were forced out of intellectual ability and skill; they came, got expressed as the journey progressed through different occurrences and stages. They all have their foundation in the experiences of travelers in scripture and the various encounters and interactions between and among others. The central idea came easily and quickly, but the structuring took a few minutes, hours, and even days, and others flowed without much thought and mental struggle.

There are those of adoration, praise, worship, healing, covering, God's caring, gratitude, mercy and grace, thanksgiving, prayer, faith, joy, conversion, deliverance, courage, determination, challenge, assurance, faithfulness, graciousness, peace, divine power, persistence, kingdom matters, redemption, hope, restoration, reconciliation, freedom, pardon and forgiveness, comfort, trust, warning, conceration, and growth.

We are all travelers and should benefit greatly from these poetic expressions.

PREFACE

THIS WORK IS A series of poems which reflect the essential attributes of God our Heavenly Father. In His dealings with human beings, and especially with His people, God always shows His character through an attribute. In many situations, He has demonstrated that He is just; that He is wise, faithful, loving, merciful, gracious, and powerful. He is also able, reliable, and trustworthy. All of God's attributes are essential to the salvation of the human beings He created. They are demonstrated in His dealings with mankind. These attributes were functional in the dealings of Christ with His disciples and the many people He encountered. The fundamental attribute that is the glue that connects all other attributes and gives meaning and value to them all is that of love. God's love came looking for us to bring grace, mercy, pardon, and power. His dealings with us who accepted His expression of love through His son Jesus carried for us the experience of the justice of God; the wisdom of God, the mercy and grace of God; the faithfulness and caring of God, and the forgiveness and power of God.

The Scripture is saturated with the experiences of men and women who enjoyed and benefited from the exercise of the attributes of God. It is the intent of the work of redemption, reconciliation, justification, sanctification, restoration, and eventually glorification that the attributes of God be internalized, manifested, demonstrated, and expressed in the lives of all those who claim His Son as Saviour and Lord. A work of renewal will be experienced as these attributes are reflected and accepted to build character as we travel.

So as you experience this effort to reveal God's attributes in His relating and dealings with mankind, it is hoped that you would have had experiences that connect you to the experiences in this work. Their names are not as important as the fact that in His name and to His glory these attributes can build the kind of character that calls attention to the internals and not simply the externals, and that the end result would be the validation of the idea that out of the heart are the issues of life. From the inside would be manifested on the outside attributes with consistency and commitment; with revelation and restoration—In His name and to His glory.

ACKNOWLEDGEMENTS

First I wish to give thanks to the Holy Spirit and the work He has done, is doing, and continues to do in my life, despite my resistance and weaknesses. I have grown in certain areas of my life and I seem stuck in other areas. Nonetheless, He continues to be patient with me. In attempting to be obedient, I have limited, or put limits on my skills and abilities for fear that I worship and praise my abilities and skills rather than the God of such gifts. I had to fully comprehend Philippians 1:6; 2:13; and 4:13. God will start something; He will commit Himself to it, and He will complete it. I have had to remember that it is God which worketh in me both <u>to will,</u> and <u>to do</u> of His good pleasure. Therefore, <u>I can</u> do all things through Christ, and His anointing, which gives me strength; which strengthens me. It is not I, but Christ, through the Holy Spirit who lives in me. The scriptures are clear, it is Jesus' anointing that breaks the joke and gives us power to get unstuck; to become free and be hopeful, and faithful. Therefore, we can do all things through His anointing because it is He who wills and does whatever needs doing through us. If we are able to accomplish anything, it would be through the anointing of Jesus by the Holy Spirit. I thank God for the Holy Spirit.

The typists who used their skills and abilities I thank, since those are not my gifts. My motto has been in every situation where there is a task to be accomplished and several persons are assigned to the tasks—"He or she who does what best, let him or her do that." Everyone can feel included, and everyone would have made a contribution. Specifically, I want to thank Ms. Jamesé Johnson who was patient, intuitive, excited, and consistent in her attitude, disposition, and diligence. I do hope she was blessed as she read in order to perform her task. Therefore, she must be credited for her personal skills and characteristics in accomplishing the technical task of structuring the poems and readying them for publication. This final project could not have been accomplished without her role being so adequately fulfilled. I am grateful to her. She has my heartfelt thanks and appreciation.

Those of you who will read, meditate upon and seek to be blessed by these poetic expressions will experience the same blessings if you ask the Holy Spirit to impress you and convict you of the message therein. Perfection was not sought, being faithful to the thought given to the truth of the message in the expression were the essential concerns. Any violation is attributed to the author alone. I am privileged and honored to have been chosen for this task especially without any formal training in writing poems and not having any other skills related to constructing poetic expressions. All I can say is: Nobody but You, Lord; Nobody but You.

Finally, the Swan collective have been my constant support and inspiration. Several years ago, my father, John Alexander Swan, gave me a copy of a poetic expression on fathering which is the lead poetic expression of this work. I want to express thanks to him for his efforts on my behalf. This work is dedicated to his memory. As a preacher in the Methodist Church, I listened to many sermons preached by my father. He was thoughtful and inspirational in his preaching. Over the years after I had grown up, although I had done some preaching on the streets at home with the Youth for Christ group in parts of the Bahamas on my own, Johnnie, as we called him, never heard me preach, until he came to the States in 1993 and he was visiting my sisters who lived in Miami, Florida. That weekend I was scheduled to be a part of a Community Health Conference and spoke to the group on that Thursday. Pastor Thomas McNelly, who was the pastor of Bethany Church heard that I would be in town, invited me to share with the congregation. My sister, Simona, dropped off our father to attend the services and this would be the first time he would hear me preach. He sat up front in the third pew and when I stood to preach, he was in full view and all through the preaching he was taking notes. This was not unusual for my dad because he was always writing. After the services were over, my sister picked us up and we went to her home to eat. Johnnie said nothing to me about the sermon which was entitled—"Don't Leave Before the Benediction." The idea was that when you leave the worship of God before the benediction, as did Judas, something might be said that would change your life and situation. Judas did not hear, but Peter did, when Jesus said, "I'm praying for you all is the proper understanding. Judas left too soon. Johnnie left the States and returned home without making any comment about the sermon I preached and the fact that he was hearing me for the first time in my denomination's church of which he had never attended. I decided, after two weeks had passed, to call and speak with him about the matter. I said Johnnie, you never said anything about the sermon and my delivery, why? There was a brief pause and he said, "Son, you did well, very well. As a matter of fact, I preached your sermon on Sunday at my church." I had the honor and privilege of preaching his eulogy in 2000 in Freeport, Bahamas to a packed church where he served. I dedicate this work to his memory.

This effort is also a tribute to my grandmother, Johnnie's mother, who took me to my first class at an early age and saw me through to the door of the school, after guiding me through the fence and stayed up with me as I did my homework. Her short stories and quick jokes would enlighten me to continue as she nodded, but would open her eyes, intuitively, to say "finish your work son." It was my grandmother who helped me understand the difference between study and homework. I thought I had studied when I completed my homework.

INTRODUCTION

WE ARE ALL TRAVELERS on this road of life. In many cases the human spirit generates the necessary inspiration to hold on and even make progress. But there are those times when there is no rain; no source of inspiration and we experience dry spots, and we seem to go from one dry place to another dry place. What is needed in cases like these are poetic expressions that inspire us to sustain until the rain. Poetic Expressions For Travelers is a creation and collection of inspirational poems that are grounded in principles of scripture and the several experiences which come from the various interactions and relationships between and among characters in the scripture. What makes them inspirational is that they carry messages that speak to people in a variety of human socio-spiritual situations. Even if they cannot enter into the experience of the expressions personally they can identify with the humanity and humanness of them in a general way. To truly enjoy each experience of each expression, the reader has to locate the context of the expression in the traveler's situation as he or she journeys. The fact is, you might be in it; coming out of it; or getting ready to go into it. At another most important level, this series of poems reflect essential attributes of God our Heavenly Father. In His dealings with human beings, and especially with his people, God always shows His character through attributes. In many situations, He has demonstrated that He is just; that He is wise, faithful, loving, merciful, powerful and kind; He is reliable too.

Put another way, these poetic expressions are inspired to inspire and to inform. They come from the lives and experiences of various persons in a variety of situations. They were challenging experiences, joyful and trusting experiences that summoned faith, trust, and faithfulness. Moods and feelings open the heart and arrest the mind and soul. Joy, sorrow, thoughts of love and kindness are real and precious. Emotions run the gamut and meet you on your journey as you travel. You are invited to relate as each core of expressions grab you where you are on the road you're traveling. You might cry, laugh, or even shout out loud when you really connect with the person inside. Be prepared and willing to go where you need to go at the very moment of your need, and your growth will be validated, reliable and satisfying so that you will pass it on in and through your life to shed light and insight on the journey of others who are traveling.

All of God's attributes are essential to the salvation of the human beings He created. They are always demonstrated in His dealings with mankind. These attributes were functional in the dealings of Christ with His disciples and the many people He encountered. The fundamental attribute that is the glue that connects all other attributes and gives values to them all is the attribute of love. God's love came looking for us bringing grace and mercy. God is love. In His dealings with sinners who accepted His love through Jesus, needed to experience the justice of God; the wisdom of God; the patience, grace and mercy, faithfulness and power of God. The word of God (scriptures) is saturated with the experiences of men and women who enjoyed and benefited from the exercise of the attributes of God. It is the intent of the work of redemption, restoration, reconciliation, justification, sanctification, and eventually glorification that the attributes of God's character be manifested, demonstrated, and internalized by all who have received Jesus as Saviour and Lord so that a work of anewal and renewal can be experienced in harmony with the work of the Holy Spirit. As these attributes are internalized they will be reflected and accepted to build characters for the kingdom and the earth made new.

So as you experience this effort to reveal God's attributes in his relating and dealings with mankind, it is hoped that you would have had encounters that connect you to the experiences of those revealed in this work. Their names are not as important as the fact that in His name and to His glory these attributes can build the kind of character that calls attention to the internals, and that the end result would be the validation of the idea that "out of the heart are the issues of life". From the inside would be the manifestation on the outside attributes with divine origin and duration with consistency and commitment with revelation and restoration. There will come a time in the life of believer-traveler, that the developed character will be tested to determine whether or not that character is developed to the point that it can stand on its own based upon prior divine input and deposits. This is why the overcoming experience is so essential and imperative. This is the reason that the believer-traveler must take advantage of every provision; every opportunity to know what the Spirit expects of us and practice obedience and compliance. The believer-traveler has to learn surrender. What if the Spirit is withdrawn and you are left without a mediator and an advocate in the heavenly count? At some point the actual work of assistance to the believer-traveler would cease and the King of Kings and Lord of Lords will make His declaration in preparation to return to welcome the believer-traveler home. Can't you hear it: "Behold I come quickly; and my reward is with me to give every man (believer-traveler) according as his work shall be".

The experience of believer-traveler, Job illustrated the point of standing alone in character. Jesus' experience in the wilderness being tempted by the devil also illustrates the point. Jesus had hid the word in His heart that He would not sin against God. His character stood alone based upon the Word; indeed He is The Word. The believer-traveler is not tempted by God as he/she travels, but He allows us to be tempted by the devil to prove to the devil that we will overcome his temptations even when we stand alone in character based upon the nature of our prior relationship with the Father, Son, and Holy Spirit, and the qualities and attributes we developed therefrom, and became infused with by God. The question to contemplate is: Why tempt Jesus and the believer-traveler when you know that the outcome was already established, even in Satan's mind. Satan quoted the scripture: "He orders His angels to protect and guard you, and they will hold you with their hands to keep you from striking your foot on a stone". You see obeying Satan's command was the issue. However, obedience of the believer-traveler belongs to God. The believer-traveler has His protection:

The Shepherd is out front leading

There is a Rod and Staff on either side.
Goodness and mercy are following you,
Everywhere Angels are watching over you day and night.
You are standing on the Rock
And you are filled with the Holy Spirit.

There is added protection and care: "The peace of God which surpasseth all understanding stands guard duty around our hearts and around our minds; in His name to His glory—Hallelujah. Nothing is allowed in unless it has the password, and that is: Jesus is Lord".

Many poems were written for public worship and praise to God; others are expressions of personal distress and suffering. These poems are written under inspiration to inspire the Travelers on the journey of life with the assurance that they are not alone; that God in the person of the Holy Spirit, decided, before their birth that if invited will take the journey with them and will order their steps and make provision for their successful arrival. So keep traveling toward your God—given promises and purposes. Treat other travelers right with understanding, forgiveness, and compassion during the journey. Acknowledge the assistance you receive from other travelers and be thankful for God's provisions during your journey. Where mercy and grace have been received, gratitude should be revealed.

Tributes

Tribute to Fathers

Written by John A. Swann Sr.

God made you fathers O so grand
God made you fathers from the master plan
His image, and likeness he gave us too
Let us ask the questions what more could he do.

He gave us a mate to help us you see
To make our life, the best it could be
We did not do well. We sin at the start
And allowed the devil to rip us apart.

God made you fathers to be loving, and kind
To not only our own, but to all that we find
That to be true and trusty let everyone know
That we work for our fathers against every foe.

Fathers your choice today, determines tomorrow's living
Make it the best to your fathers, the life you are giving
You cannot go wrong, if you give him your best.
That's all he asks of us fathers, He'll do the rest.

He'll mould you, and make you, as the potter does clay
He'll teach you, train, you, in your fathers way.
Committed faithful to wife, children and friends
That's the only way God our father understands.

On your knees with them, teach them what to say
To God our heavenly Father for this is the right way
He asks us to be faithful strong constant not to fear
For he promises to be with fathers always, everywhere.

A father was made to be patient and kind
This should be constant always in mind
Sing Alleluia to our father who came and
Gave us victory, in His only son's name.

Give thanks to our father, thanks to the son
Give thanks to the Holy Spirit, fathers three in one
We praise, we worship, magnify and adore
By his grace and his mercy let us love fathers more.

Mother—One Who Really Cares

The one who bears the sweetest name
And adds luster to the same.
Long life to her for there's no other
Who takes the place of a dear Mother.

Someone who takes the time to listen.
Who lends a helping hand,
And makes you feel secure, by always
Being there as planned.
No other, but a gracious Mother.

Someone who knows your special needs,
And seeks to give you inner strength.
She gives her all, she wants to please,
Through words as well as deeds.

Someone who takes a special interest,
In just how well you're faring.
It's time to tell, and for her to hear,
Mom, thank you so much for caring.

L.O.V.E.

L is for loyalty,
O is to open your heart.
V are the vows you promise to keep.
E is for an everlasting relationship.

A. Renee Turner

Hair

The hair aren't real,
So it wasn't a deal.
The wig is on her head.
She needs to lay that thing to bed.

She whips her hair from side to side,
When she gets on the exercise ride.
He hair shifts and glides,
But it seems to give her great pride.

Her ponytail is like a fairy tale,
Not real.
Stop lying to yourself young girl.
Be real, be true, would you!

A. Renee Turner

Around Me

The trees and daisies are blooming.
The old folks are brooming.

The babies are crawling.
The teenagers are brawling.

I'm writing about my troubles.
The words flow on the double.

The people around me are
Whispering in my ear.
I try not to hear.
The words they are dishing out.

They bring on my face a long frown.
The kids around me are saying
This and that
Saying things that aren't facts.

A. Renee Turner

1

Adoration—Assurance—Coverage—Covering

You

You are Holy.
You are Righteous.
You are Awesome.
You are Creator, Lord, and King.

You are Sovereign.
You're Almighty.
You are Gracious.
You are Savior, Redeemer, Friend.

You are Mercy.
You are Love.
You are Joy.
You are Protector, Provider, Peace.

You are Alpha.
You are Omega.
You are everything in between.
You are Father, Son, and Holy Ghost.

You are Powerful.
You are Magnificent.
You're the great I am.
You are Jehovah, Father, God.

God Is

God is Savior
God is Lord
God is Faithful
God is Merciful
God is Gracious
God is Love
God is Redeemer
God is King of Kings
God is Lord of Lords
God is Helper
God is Teacher
God is Friend
God is Master
God is Father
God is Protector
God is Provider
God is Truth
God is a Giver
God is Strong
God is Almighty
God is Sovereign
God is Creator
God is Sustainer
God is God

Faithful Is He

You are so faithful
To those who claim You as Father
You are so faithful
To those who trust Your Word.

You are so faithful
In all situations, good and bad
You are so faithful
I'm made happy and glad.

You are so faithful
We can rest assured in Thee
You are so faithful
With Your mercy, grace and peace.

I trust you now
I trust you then
You are so faithful
I'll trust You when.

Lift Him Up

Lift Him up ye saints of God,
In his words of adulation.
Praise His name and sacrifice
In thankful admiration.

Lift Him up those called to serve,
With deeds of appreciation.
Those in need He gives through you,
And knows no hesitation.

Lift Him up ye called of God,
To love without reservation.
Let His peace go out to all,
In courageous exaltation.

Lift Him up all ye redeemed,
With songs of celebration.
Sing His praises far and near,
In grateful adoration.

Lift Him up ye warriors,
In prayers and meditation.
He will bless you from on High,
In holy consecration.

Lift Him up, Oh Lift Him Up.
Let His Spirit work through you.
Give Him the glory, Give Him the Praise
Hallelujah, our voices raise.

Thank You Lord For Everything

Thank You Lord for Who You Are.
Thank You Lord for What You Did.
Thank You Lord Your Gift to Me.
Thank You Lord for Everything.

Thank You Lord for Love so Sure
Thank You Lord for Grace so Pure.
Thank You Lord for Saving Me.
Thank You Lord for Everything.

Thank You Lord for Faith and Peace.
Thank You Lord for Joy that never Cease.
Thank You Lord for upholding me.
Thank You Lord for Everything.

Thank You Lord for righting the Wrong.
Thank You Lord for being so Strong.
Thank You Lord for guiding Me.
Thank You Lord for Everything.

I just want to Thank You.
I just want to Thank You.
I just want to Thank You.
Thank You Lord for Everything.

He'll Never Leave You

He will never leave you to wonder
You'd do that on your own
He will not have you to falter
That comes with doing your thing.
From Strength to strength, He bids you stride
His guidance, His power you can abide.

Don't ask Him for the storms to cease
They will your faith to try
Don't ask for traits to away
They keep your feet from going astray
Don't ask for mountains to be brought low
Just ask for strength to climb aglow.

Trust His work, hear Him say
My child I'll never leave
Nor will I ere forsake
Keep trusting in what's promised
My Word I will obey.

So Glad You Came

I'm so pleased you came for me.
I'm so happy you die for me.
I'm so glad you rose for me.
You cared, you came to see about me.

I'm so glad you saved my soul.
I'm so pleased you made me whole.
I'm so happy you cleansed my life.
You came, you stayed to set me free.

I'm so happy you left for Heaven.
I'm so glad you're my advocate and mediator.
I'm so pleased you're representing me.
You care about my soul's salvation.

I'm so pleased you're coming back for me.
I'm so happy you've forgiven me.
I'm so glad you rescued me.
You care, you promise forever with you.

I'm so glad.
I'm so pleased.
I'm so happy.
You cared and delivered me.

Men of Courage

Men of Courage, do not falter
When their foe is big and strong.
Men of courage, do not stumble,
Through the path is rough and thorned.
Courage gives them fortitude.
Courage makes them bold.

Men of courage do not waiver,
When the winds of strife doth blow.
Men of courage struggle onward.
Finding strength for every stroke.
Courage is their ever watch word.
Courage fills their soul.

Men of courage know their Helper,
When their knees begin to buckle.
Standing by them is their Savior
Ready to share their heavy load.
Onward upward God has called us.
Never to miss the well—lit road.

It takes courage, men of honor.
God expects us to endure.
When He sees us in our struggle.
He has promised to give us more.
When He yokes up in our effort.
Men of courage we will soar.

God Is God

God can give, and God can take
God can make, and God can break
God puts up, and God takes down
God is God.

God is God
Sister and Brother
God is God
There's none other
God is God.

God sets up kings, and queens dethrone
God comforts saints, God confronts sin
God fulfills dreams and victories win
God is God.

God is mercy, and God is just
God is Creator, we can trust
God is faithful, kind, and true
God is God.

God has no beginning, God has no end
God has no limit, God has no when
God is the greatest, God is all
God is God.

When I Say

When I say Master, My sorrows disappear.
When I say Father, He drives away my fears.
When I say Savior, My blinded eyes can see.
When I say Jesus, He speaks peace to me.

When you say Savior, He always gives an ear.
When you say help me, He guides from every snare.
When you say praise Him, His name is glorified.
When you say Jesus, He speaks peace to you.

When we say Spirit, He opens up our eyes.
When we say pardon, He points us to the sky.
When we say mercy, He represents our prayer.
When we say Spirit, He brings hope and cheer.

When The Waters Are Troubled

When the waters of my life are troubled,
I do not need a bridge.
My waters are so badly raging.
No bridge will ever do.

He calms the storms, He paths the sea.
He raises the dead, and heals the lame.
He sights the blind, He hears the deaf,
He can be a bridge but is much more than that.

God's not about just being a bridge.
He'd rather speak to raging waves.
He does not want us just to cope.
That's what a bridge will do.

God always has a greater plan.
Then that we ask of Him.
He sees before we need His help.
And knows just what to send.

So if you think you need a bridge,
For troubles in your life,
Don't ask the Lord a bridge to build
Ask Him the troubled waters still.

He Covered Me

I was clean and safe within.
No worry, no trouble just free to sore.
But once I left my father's home,
My way was marred with doubts and bore.

At first my world was fun galore.
I partied hard, and partied some more.
But when compared with what I left,
My thoughts and heart had wondered back.

Trouble came and surrounded me.
Faith was summoned my step to free.
But faith was clear, although you're blue.
I won't take you around, I'll take you through.

My resolve was firm, my steps were swift.
I was never sure what Dad would do.
But as I moved closer to home,
I could feel his presence and hear his grown.

With arms outstretched he gave embrace.
His smile was broad, his hands quite firm.
My odered smell did fill the air.
But he did not ask, why, when, or where.

He covered me, He covered me.
Now safe and free from sin.
He covered me, He covered me.
Fresh and delivered, I'm clean within.

He covered me, He covered me.
Although unclean, He covered me.
My faults unseen, my sins forgiven.
All praise to God, He covered me.

Cover Me

Cover me, Cover me
I am naked
Cover me
Sin and shame
Have exposed me
Lord, I need you, to
Cover me.

Let Your righteousness
Cover me, Cover me
When I'm clean and,
When I'm not
Cover me, Cover me
Savior, I need You, to
Cover me.

I need Your mercy
And Your grace.
Cover me
Your peace and favor
Are in place
But Cover me,
Cover me
Let my life be
Covered by Thee.

Cover me, Cover me
Lord I pray You'd
Cover me
Let nothing be seen
Of me I do pray
Master I beech You,
Cover me.

Faithful Is God

Faithful is God to His children.
Faithful is He to His own.
Faithful is God when in trouble
Fighting to be His alone.

Faithful is God to His promises
Made to His children in faith
Whatever you need is in storage
Released when you trust Him and pray.

Faithful is God to His purpose
Faithful is God to His call
And faithful is God to revelation
But more faithful is He to His Word.

God is Worthy

*Praise God, Praise God
God is worthy to be praised, oh
Praise God, Praise God
God is worthy to be praised.*

*Hallelujah, Hallelujah
God is worthy to be praised, oh
Hallelujah, Hallelujah, God is worthy
To be praised.*

*Magnify Him, Magnify Him
God is worthy to be praised, oh
Glorify Him, Glorify Him,
God is worthy to be praised.*

*Give Him Honor, Give Him Honor
God is worthy to be praised
All the honor and glory
God is worthy to be praised.*

In His Presence

In His Presence
I have peace and tranquility.
In His Presence
I have healing and deliverance.
In His presence
I am safe forever more.

In His Presence
You have grace and mercy.
In His Presence
There is victory and so sweet.
In His Presence
There's celebration and joy.

In His Presence
We have the assurance of salvation.
In His Presence
We have it all.
In His Presence
We will never not really fall.

Until It Rains

If you are experiencing drought in your life
Drought of any kind
Spiritual, financial, social, or whatever
There is a good word from the Lord.

With all the stuff we're going through
We wonder how we'll make it
But the Word of God is faithful and true
Until the rain, God will sustain.

Rains will come, but until they do
You will not run out of what you need
For the promise of God Word is
Until it rains, I will sustain.

Rains will come in God's own time
For trouble don't last always
So hold on to His Word for after He sustains
He'll send down the rains.

You may have to go to a water brook
And the brook may even dry up
You may have to go from one dry place to another
But God will sustain, until it rains.

2

Conversion—Challenge—Concecration—Christian Growth

I Met The Savior

Like a ship upon the ocean,
Tossed to and fro by the waves
Was my life without the Savior,
And my Soul before He saved.

Oh the path was rough and thorny
And the way seemed dark and dreary.
But oh, one day I met the Savior
My Jesus, yes He cares.

I met the Savior
So can you
I met the Savior
Kind and true
I met the Savior
Shipwreck and blue
I met the Savior
So can you

He has found me, He can find you
When the tide of life is high
Just be faithful my dear brother
There's a crown beyond the sky.

New Life

New Life in Jesus,
That's the first step.
A gift from the Father,
Assurance to get through.

New life with others,
Disciples as you.
Given to oneness,
All the way through.

Come offer New Life,
To those by the Way
Tell them who sent You
To help them come through.

Come all with New Life
There's work to be done
Inside and Outside
He'll see us all through.

New Life in Jesus
New Life from God
Filled with His Spirit
We'll make the journey through.

What About The Rest Of Me

I know that I'm not perfect,
I know I have some faults.
I see the spot and your assaults,
But what about the rest of me?

I'm under reconstruction,
A spot I'm sure you'll glean.
He'll wash and wash and make me clean,
Until its like the rest of me.

You will not know the rest of me,
By looking at the spot.
You see my spot, that's not a lot,
For there is all the rest of me.

Our call is to be spotless,
No matter what it takes.
A spot will show, no stain it makes,
So why not see the rest of me.

Condemn me not because the spot,
Is there this very hour.
He gives me faith and cleansing power
Because he sees the rest of me.

Take out the mote, remove the plank,
And help me on my way.
By looking at the rest of the clay,
We all can glow, and grow, and pray.

The Armor

Sober we are, Sober we must be,
We're in the Army of the Lord.
We are not of the night, we are of the day.
Ready to defend the faith.

Breastplate of faith and love.
Helmet of hope and salvation
We're not destined for wrath
But for obtaining salvation.

However, whether awake or asleep
We'll reign with the King
No more separation from Him
Our Lord Jesus Christ our Savior.

Then wear your Armor well
Every demon in the hell will tell
The banner under which your labor
God the Father, God the Holy Spirit and God
The begotten Son.

When God Has His Day

God is about to have a day
He had a few days before
When sin and sinners get out of hand
God will show His hand.

Noah was given a task to build
An Ark of Safety to all who would so in
The message of destruction and doom went forth
But no response gave God His first day.

The door was shut an action divine
No one could get in, no one could get out
As the drops of rain began to fall
Those outside began to question their call.

They had the chance of 120 years
They jeered; they scorned and had their fun.
But the door was shut
Their doom was sealed for sure
A simple yes to the word being preached
Could have been the choice of all
But instead, the rain fell, the flood came
Eight were saved, the rest were lost.

The Will of God

May the Will of God always be the Will in Me
May the eyes of God be those through which I see
May the Will of God be the Will in Me
And my will be lost in Thine.

May the mind of God always be the mind in Me
May the words I speak of, be the words of Thee
May the mind of God be the mind in Me
And my thoughts be those of Thine.

May the peace of God always be the peace in Me
May the grace of God be that of which I seek
May the peace of God be the peace in Me
And my life be fused in Thine.

May the love of God always be the love in Me
May I share His love wherever I may be
May the Love of God be manifest in Me
And His name be Glorified.

Modeling The Model

I have to Model Jesus.
He is the Word made flesh.
I have to model from His Word
His character's there to bless.

I know no other model
Who gave His life for me
Who left His Throne in glory,
From sin to set me free.

No Model is so perfect.
His example is so clear.
His spirit makes us willing,
To model Him with cheer.

A modeling school His church must be,
To help us on our way.
His presence will be felt by all,
Who are willing to obey.

We lift Him up in word and deed.
His mission shall succeed.
His Spirit has the drawing power
To work through those who Model Him.

No Time To Look At Me

The time is late to look around.
And watch the lives of those you see.
Their lives are not a mirror be.
And please don't look at me.

The time is past to look at self.
And think that all is well.
You may not see what Jesus sees.
No time to think you're swell.

The time is now to look above,
With hope, and joy, and glee.
His promise is to come in love
No time to run and flee.

Look in the Word, and keep the view,
Of Him who died for thee.
Don't look around, don't look at self.
And please, don't look at me.

Observations From The Back Of The Church

It's hard to see when you're up front
What those up front are doing.
But when you take a seat at back
All things are brought to view.

No central theme defines the praise.
Alternatives not even raised.
Routine, Routine is all you see.
As if nothing else can be.

All seem stuck in religious rot
Which stifles all that's good.
They get so busy having church.
The church they fail to be
No one leads out in giving praise.
The way the Bible says.
The praise is dry and has no life.
Is dead and goes no where.

The worship follows the same each time,
They gather to begin.
To be spontaneous is a sin,
And frowned on from within.

The scripture, prayer and song don't match
The sermon does not connect.
Too many fractions will appear,
The pews left so confused.

Don't go up front, stay in the back.
Until the front can see.
The tortures that routine can bring,
And sense why others flee

Where is the Lamb in all of this.
In Heaven the fronters think
He wants to come and be apart
Where praise and thanksgiving ring.

But oh we need to make a change
From routine to be free
To worship, praise, and bless His name
So the Lamb can come and be.

Trapped in Habits of Sin

We oft should tell our children
Don't start what they must stop.
The risk of its continuing
Might ultimately be their lot.

A thought you have, a behavior makes
A behavior made, a habit formed.
A habit formed, a character gained.
Your life can experience unnecessary pain.

Being trapped is not a freedom move
In bondage, can't you see
That's not the way to live your life
I would for Jesus be.

No habit of sin should be so strong
To trap you in its grip
Don't start a thought that paves its path
You're not that wise, you're not that smart.

Yet all is not for nought I say,
For here's a special word.
I know of one, a habit breaker,
He is the Lord, the great Creator.

He loves us so that once He died,
To take away our sins
They hung Him High, no reason why,
He died and rose with pride.

Oh yes He rose and went on high,
To seal a place for me.
To be with Him forever more,
Thank God, Bless God I'm free.

The Wilderness Experience

The wilderness is a special place
Where God shapes our thinking
Moses, David, and Jesus Christ
Benefited from a wilderness experience.

What is this matter of the wilderness
Is it in the wild of life?
It is a sense of the isolation
From the things and people that count.

Great lessons can be learned
In the wilderness of life
You're there to learn where no place else
Could teach you the imperatives.

It could be social, mental, or psychological
It could be physical, financial, or spiritual
Whatever the realm, it's not a shame
Your experience will surely tell you when.

Learn what you must and well
The lessons learned can be humbling
Denial of those things vital to life
Confirms your confidence and trust in God.

Your trust in God is imperative
That's learned by your wilderness experience
The flesh is subdued and denied
By faith and truth you live.

When you don't know God that wilderness
Your drawing experience is sure
For God's desire is to teach you how
To make your experience benefit for good.

Baptize and Fill Me

Baptize me Lord,
With the gift of the Holy Spirit.
Fill me with His power,
T o live and glorify (You) Thee.

Fill me with your Spirit,
For the journey Lord.
His need is for every hour.
With Him every day's a joy.

The gift of the Holy Spirit,
Is given to those in need.
The assurance of a Savior,
Who died from Sin to Save.

The filling of the Holy Spirit,
Will give you power within.
To live and give God glory,
For the victory He brings.

Grow In Love

We have to make progress as Christians
Overcoming is our measure of success
Heaven and earth made over
Is the home of the victorious rest.

Our growth must take place in love
The love that God has for us
He says in His Word that He is love
When we embrace Him we grow in grace.

We increase in God
When we increase in love
Love frees us to love unconditionally
We must grow and develop in Him.

The love of God is foundation
For all that we do in His name
Love develops us out of selfishness
What I do the least I do to Him.

From Riches to Rags to Riches

He came to earth
From riches to rags
Perfect was He
No sin, and no guile
A model was He
In Word and in deed
He's our salvation
Redeemer is He.

Job was all human
But perfect was he
This was the declaration
Of God about him
From riches to rags
His experience you'll see
Didn't stop Satan
From stealing from him.

There's restoration
In Jesus, you'll see
Job's faithful endurance
Was counted for good
More than he realized
Was given to him
More children, more riches
And content, delight.

Hide the Word

We overcome evil by the Word.
Temptations are met with the Word.
Power is gained by the Word.
Just hide the Word in your heart.

Victories are ours through the Word.
Strengths are renewed in the Word.
Hopes are realized by the Word.
Just hide the Word in your heart.

Weaknesses are defeated with the Word.
Self is dethroned by the Word.
Praises are expressed through the Word.
Just hide the Word in your heart.

Resist the devil with the Word.
Review God's promises in the Word.
Thy Word have I hide in my heart.
Just hide the Word in your heart.

Keep on your lips God's Word.
Obedience is achieved through God's Word.
Grace and Mercy are extended in God's Word.
Just hide the Word in your heart.

3

Comfort—Deliverance—Determination—Divine Power

The Great Exchange

Justified by faith in Jesus.
Without the deeds of the Law.
Redemption and Pardon.
What a wonderful exchange.

His righteousness for our righteousness.
Right standing before our God.
Guilt cancelled with restoration.
What a marvelous exchange.

Transgressions all forgiven.
Jesus the Christ our substitute.
The transgressor is given a perfect record.
This is the good news of the exchange.

Your death for my life.
My earth for Your Heaven.
My poverty for Your riches.
What an unselfish exchange.

Talk about the good news.
Jesus stands in our stead.
Pleading our cases to the Father.
What a redemptive exchange.

Glory to the Father.
Glory to the Son.
Glory to the Holy Spirit.
Three is One
Just for me.

Claim It

Claim God's forgiveness from the Throne
It is available to one and all
Claim His pardon for your sins
God is anxious, It's Jesus' will.

Claim God mercies offered to all
In times of repentance when the Holy Ghost calls
Given in love, gentle and true
God is compassionate faithful to me.

Claim God's grace secured by the Lord
Free to all who ask with sincere delight
Given in great measure all that you need
Reconciliation, Restoration, with grateful appeal.

God will forgive you He promised to
If you seek, you will find, ask and receive
Nothing can hinder your surrender to Him
God is our Father, His children are we.

Claim His deliverance full and complete
Get attached to His power supreme
His gracious attention His desire to save
All those who embrace redemption story.

Our God Sees Before

Our God has prevision.
He sees everything before.
We function as His children in the Now.
He can function in the not yet.

Trust Him with your cares.
Trust Him with your life.
He might function where you are.
He'll function where you're not.

You may not see Him working.
If what's to be done is not near you.
He knows where you are headed.
He works where you plan to be.

No matter what you see or not see.
He works for your good when He moves.
No matter the problem, no matter the pain.
He will be there none the same.

He'll move at the time you move.
He'll move at Twilight if you move at Twilight.
He will move to where the problem is.
And the not yet becomes the no longer.

His move will set you free indeed
From worry, doubt, and fear.
He knows your pain, He knows your care.
His grace and favor will fill the air.

To Be Happy—Attitudes

If you have been set free from sin, Be Happy.
If you are no longer a slave to sin, Be Happy.
If you are no longer in bondage to sin, Be Happy.

If you've accepted Jesus as Savior, Be Happy.
If you have allowed Him to be your Lord, Be Happy.
If the Holy Spirit is directing your life, Be Happy.

If it is your desire and willingness to follow His guidance, Be Happy.
If you are married to Jesus and will no longer also date the devil, Be Happy.
If you have presented your body a living sacrifice and taken your hand off of it, Be Happy.

If you have been freed from the deception of the enemy, Be Happy.
If when you met Jesus you had little or nothing and now have everything in Him, Be Happy.
If you are living in right standing with God the Father, Be Happy.

If your name is written in the Lambs Book of Life, Be Happy.
If you know your sins and transgressions have been forgiven, Be Happy.
If you are busy doing what you can in His vineyard to hasten His return, Be Happy.

The Blood Cries Out

(Genesis 4:10)

From Africa to the Americas
From Homeland to the then New World
In waters shallow and deep
The blood of Blacks cries out for Justice.

From careless acts of capture
To brutal behavior in transport
Chains of denials and oppression of the Spirit
The blood of Blacks cries out for freedom.

On plantations owned by cruel men
The toil was inhumane and barbaric
Day and night no escape in sight
The blood of Blacks cries out for liberation.

The justice sought, the freedom talked
Was met with hostility, and violence
No one would hear liberation's ring
But the blood cried out for redemption.

The injustice of death, handling and treatment
The blood stained streets and allies
The imperfect justice metered out in human courts
Has not stopped the cries of the blood.

America, blood is on your hands
For the life of the slain is in the blood
The voices of the blood of every unjust stain
Cry out today from their graves.

No matter how hard it is or seem,
To see and understand now
God will make every wrong right
In His time in response to the cry.

We have seen injustice and pain
We have been victims of the same
But we have been promised
The avenging of the blood that cries.

What have you done America?
The voices of black blood cry out
From the sea and from the land
The blood of blacks cries out all around.

We trust God because He has promised,
Ultimate and righteous justice
That is so lacking and hard to find
We hear the blood cry out from the ground

Our blood cries out for justice
Our blood cries out for fairness
Our blood cries out for restitution
Our blood cries out from the ground.

Life According to the Spider: Crawling, Cracks, And Clinging

Proverbs 30:24-28

In the King's palace she finds her place
No one assisted her there.
She crawled, she cracked and now she clings.
Holding on to what success brings.

Our lives are much the Spider be,
Committed to succeed.
We have to crawl and look for cracks
We've got the help to cling.

He gives us strength to crawl.
He gives us wisdom to see cracks.
He gives us commitment to cling
And power to hold on.

Knocked down sometimes but we're crawling
Up against the wall but looking for cracks
Some try to pull us down but we're clinging.
He gives us power to hold on.

Buffeted at times but we're crawling
Doors are closed but we're looking for cracks
Slipping and sliding but we're clinging
We have the power to hold on.

We're crawling in Jesus Name
We're finding cracks through the Word
We're clinging with Holy Ghost power
He gives us strength to hold on.

I must learn how to crawl
You must understand learn how to see cracks
We must have commitment to cling
Lord help us all to hold on.

Lessons from the Spider,
Teach us how to live.
Crawling, Cracks, and Clinging
There's no other way to win.
God gives the power to hold on.

Thank God we know how to crawl.
Bless Jesus we understand how to see cracks.
Praise the Holy Spirit for the power to cling
Glory Hallelujah there's safety in the King's palace.

Value and Worth

I have value, I have worth
No more questions, no more doubts
Celebrate these virtues from above,
For my value, and my worth.

I have purpose for my being.
Divinely given I do esteem.
Forward always, destiny driven.
Hopeful, grateful, vision seen.

Nurtured by confidence, determination supreme,
Internal strength propels my dreams.
Courage to face my every challenge,
Victorious living my only means.

I have value and I have worth,
Cannot be erased I know their birth.
Offered to all who would receive,
Come unto Me is the great appeal.

No Matter What
I Will Trust in God

I will trust You no matter what.
I will trust You come what may.
Storms may come, Winds will blow.
I will trust You all the way.

All the way I'll trust You.
Morning, noon, and night
In the darkness of my experience
I will trust You with delight.

In my trials and temptations
No more doubting, no more fear.
I will trust Your promise of deliverance.
The enemy will try and surely dare.

I'm determined to always trust You.
In the fire and in the flamed
I will testify of Your power
If not rescued, even if not claimed.

You are Sovereign in Your Action.
You are Lord and God of all.
Trusting always in Your Mercy
Almighty, Faithful, Righteous God.

God Protects His Own

Surely God will deliver
From the snares of the enemy
From his attacks and his schemes
God will protect seen and unseen.

With His feathers He will cover
Under His wings you can trust
You will not fear the terror
By day and neither by night.

Thousands shall fall at thy side
Ten thousand at thy right hand
But no evil shall come near you
For God will protect His own.

I shall make the Lord my refuge
My strength He shall always be
No evil shall therefore befall me
Nor come near my dwelling place.

No More Bleeding,
Not Another Drop

Twelve years she suffered,
And shed many a tear.
But determination and purposed in her heart
No more bleeding, not another drop.

She spent all the money acquired
But no cure was ever found.
Her hopes seemed to ware,
As she suffered severe pain.

But she heard about Jesus,
And His power to cure and heal.
Sickness and illness private and revealed,
Those who had faith, and only believed.

The crowd around Him did not discourage.
She kept her eyes fixed on Him.
To get just close in position,
To make contact with His holy Being.

He knew she was pressing her way
And persisting by faith to connect.
He delayed, slowed down, and even stopped
For her plan to take hold by just a touch.

Finally she reached His presence,
And stretched out her hand expectantly.
In hope to reach the hem of His garment,
Wishing not to be seen or even felt.

But her touch of faith brought wholeness,
And immediately she sought to escape.
But Jesus called out to her witness,
For a testimony of Thanksgiving and praise.

He felt the touch when virtue left,
To do its work although unseen.
For this persistent child of God
To proclaim a realized and fulfilled dream.

No more bleeding, not another drop.
Was her testimony on the spot.
I thank you for caring and making me whole
And allowing me to experience new birth in my soul.

I Don't Look Like What I've Been Through

I've been through many ups and downs
More downs than ups I'm sure
But grace and mercy is on my side
Thank God I'm not what I've been.

What can I say about a God
Who cares so much for me
He sees you through the darkest hour
And protects you by His love.

He finds you in the biggest mess
And cleans you day by day
He's patient, kind, and compassionate
His guiding hand is real.

He brought me through suffering and pain
The consequence of sin
I'm thankful, grateful, and satisfied
I'm blessed beyond belief.

You see me now not like I was
I'm different than before
I wear His name, I'm made brand new
I don't look like what I've been through.

4

Faith—Faithfulness—God's Caring—Graciousness

Speaking God's Word

Speak, God's Word, into your life
And into the life of others.
The power of the Word will change your life
And give you peace within.

Speak, God's Word, over your home
And all who dwell therein.
Father, Mother, Children, All
Will experience the power to live.

Speak, God's Word, over your friends,
Acquaintance one and all.
When the Word's sent forth in any form
It'll accomplish all that God intends.

He Will Sustain

The Word of God is true
There's drought on every hand
We expect rain from You
Before the rain, God will sustain

Rain will come, but until it does
You will not run out of your needs
For the promise of God is that
Until it rains, He will sustain

Until it rains, overcome your fear
Until it rains obey God in Faith
Until it rains celebrate His goodness
He will sustain, until it rains

Testify of His faithfulness
Tell of His mercy and grace
His promises are sure
Until it rains, He will sustain

Rain is sure to come
For trouble don't last always
But until it rains God will sustain
And after He sustains, He will send rain

Faithfulness

Faithfulness in the small things
Is preparation sure
Faithfulness in simple matters
Is preparation some more.

Acts of faithfulness everyday
Builds a faithful character
Decisions, choices small and big
Prepare you for a great reward.

Being faithful to our God
In small things, and in the big
Gives evidence everyday that
They both go with each other.

You can't have one without the other
God wants to give you both
Your faithfulness in the small things
Will lead to faithfulness in much.

God Gives Us

God gives us hope and encouragement
Whenever He sees our sadness.
God gives us grace and mercy,
To allow us to express our gladness.

God gives us peace and joy,
Whenever He knows our sorrow.
God gives us knowledge and wisdom,
To be strong and survive till tomorrow.

God gives us courage and faith,
Whenever we begin to start doubting.
God gives us love and compassion,
To keep us from resorting to pouting.

God gives is forgiveness and redemption
Whenever we fall short of His glory
God gives us promises of assurance
To keep us hopeful and holy.

God Gets The Glory

Satan was jealous that he
Could not create
So he bad mouth God to His creatures
Some of them bought it and others did not
But he got many to question God
And His Being.

God was so merciful, God was
So great
He gave them time to change
Their beliefs
But Satan had deceived them
And blinded their eyes
From all God's goodness and His
Creative powers.

Some came to their senses
As pleas were sent forth
Satan resisted along with his crowd
But others repented and were
Reconciled and restored.

Satan got kicked out
Of heaven and home
He had a following who
Also got expelled soon,
Only after they insisted
To follow his lead
Into a pit of hell and doom.

Worship the Father, Son, and
The Spirit
Creatures created cannot
Claim it as their own
They were never created or made
To their glory
A heaven, an earth and
All creation story.

God is Creator, no other but He
Has all of the power to save
And make whole
Let's give Him the glory, majesty
And praise
For all of His goodness, though
All His own
Sharing as He does, His riches
And His Throne.

God's Moral Law

He spoke them
Then He wrote them
With His own finger
He scripted them on pillows of stone

His character they reveal
They represent His seal
So in their heart
He plants them

They express His love
So direct and clear
For Him as God
And for our fellow men

Love for God
Need love from God
Love for Mankind
Requires love for self

Love is our God
The law our objectives
A focus on God
And a focus on us.

The law of love
The law of direction
Points us to the Savior
The gift to Mankind.

Sow Into Others

Sow into others the Word of God
No other internals will do
The work of character building
So needed so giving, so true.

Sow into others the kindness
That comes only from above
Let it reflect from within you
Easy, and loving.

Sow into others compassion
That flows from a life of content
So confident with your walk with the Savior
For others, whether big or small

Sow into others forgiveness
Experience it all over again
The love of God, and the Savior
From Heaven to earth the same.

Tell God You're Sorry

Tell God you're sorry
If you really mean it
So many times it's just talk
But actions speak louder than words.

Tell God you're sorry
For all the wrong you've done
He might send you to others
Who suffered from your offense.

Tell God you're sorry
From Him you'll garner strength
To cease from sin and foolish acts
That disregard His holy name.

Tell God you're sorry
Come what may
He'll meet you at repentance
His grace you will receive.

Restore The Joy

My sin has separated me,
From my Lord, my God.
I can't go on without knowing,
My joy will/has been restored.

So selfish in my actions.
No thought I gave to Thee.
My Lord and Savior always,
My joy restore to me.

Oh gracious Heavenly Father,
I bow my heart in shame.
You warned me of distractions,
I have myself to blame.

Gracious Holy Spirit,
Help me as I try.
To learn how to sing again,
To learn how to praise.

The Testimony of the Sheep

The Lord is my shepherd
His sheep said to me
Come and be led by the Savior
He's gentle, He's patient, come see.

I've gone astray on occasion
He searches until He finds
Me wandering away from His presence
So kindly and warm His embrace.

Come with Me He says with Intention
To return me to the fold
Of safety and protection from the enemy
My being is so precious to Him.

I'm so glad that I have a good shepherd
Who gives me attention each day
I promised to never displease Him
No matter what comes my way.

The leader is my shepherd
His rod and staff my companions be
Goodness and mercy do follow
And the Spirit comforts me.

5

Gratitude—Healing— Hope—Joy

Love Has No Stones to Throw

Love has no stones to throw at those,
Caught, and trapped in Satan's snares.
Stones are thrown by Pharisees, and Scribes
Who cannot see.

Their eyes are clogged with logs and planks
Their hearts are filled with glee.
When those accused and condemned, are thrown at Jesus' feet

And there they kneel in simple faith,
Their sins exposed to thee
No word of harsh reproof is heard,
Just sounds of sweet relief.

Thy sins are now forgiven child,
Stand up and go thy way.
And as you go and sin no more
No stones are thrown I say.

For he who seeks to throw a stone,
His life must perfect be.
No mote, or plank is in his eyes,
He can but perfect see.

Look at your life, examine it,
Be careful with your view
The one who seeks to snare us all
Has devious plans for you.

Love is forgiving
Love is kind
Love is merciful
Love is sublime
Love is humble
Love is a—glow
Love has no stones to throw

Gifts From Heaven

Gifts are small, gifts are large.
Gifts are regular, gifts are a blast.
Gifts are short lived, gifts can last.
Gifts from Heaven have eternal class.

The gift of the Word will light your path.
The gift of the Word can make you see.
The gift of the Word will help you walk right.
The gift from Heaven is lamp, light, and sight.

The gift of the Spirit counselor divine.
The gift of the Spirit replacing the Son.
The gift of the Spirit is available to all.
The gift from Heaven is perfect for the toil.

The gift of the Lamb salvation assured.
The gift of the Lamb man to God restored.
The gift of the Lamb all sins are forgiven.
This gift from Heaven was indeed love driven.

The gift of eternal life made possible by Him.
The gift of eternal life what a gift God would share.
The gift of eternal life so gracious so bold.
This gift from Heaven satisfies the soul.

He Took The Cup

He took the cup,
It was a bitter cup.
He took the cup,
It was a dirty cup.
He took it for you.
He took it for me.

I had a sin cup,
So did you.
I could not drink my cup,
Neither could you.
But Jesus came, and
He took the cup.

Bitter and Dirty,
He took the cup.
Shameful and Painful,
He took the cup.
Weighed down by sorrow,
He took the cup.

He took the cup.
He took the cup.
Thank God for Jesus,
He took the cup.
No other could save us,
In Heaven or on Earth,
Thank you dear Savior,
For taking the cup.

Thy Kingdom Come

The Kingdom of Heaven is at hand.
John came preaching loudly.
The Kingdom of Heaven is at hand.
John kept teaching firmly.

Thy Kingdom come, He taught them.
His disciples heard Him say.
Thy Kingdom come, Thy will be done,
In Heaven as well as on the Earth.

Thy Kingdom is in Heaven.
There's a Kingdom within the heart.
Come reign and rule, put on your crown.
I submit my will to thine.

Our Lord's Appeal: Lean On Me

Lean on Me
When you're not strong
You'll need someone
That you can hold on
I'll give you strength
To make it through
I died for you
I'll get you over.

Just lean on Jesus
Lean on you Savior
Just trust His word
You'll get the victory
It'll bring you success

Lean on His word
He is a friend
That stickest closer
Than any brother
He'll see you through
All of your sorrows
He has the plans
To bring you over

Just call the Savior
He'll hear your plea
Call for His power
He'll share His Might
And deliver you.

They Too Shall Pass

Life has so many problems,
They come in every class.
This one here, and this one there,
But, they too shall pass.

They come so unexpected,
They come sometimes in mass.
They have no time or place to strike,
But, they too shall pass.

They last at times, a moment,
They sometimes last for days.
They block our paths and halt our ways,
But, they too shall pass.

They have no strength to keep us down,
They give us cause to pray.
When we say Lord, have Thine own way,
Then, they too shall pass.

Koinonia

No fellowship so sweet so dear,
As that with Christ our Lord.
No fellowship so rich and pure,
His presence you'd adore.
Give Him your heart, your soul, your all
And fellowship, this is His call.

Come fellowship with Jesus,
His voice so sweet and clear.
Come fellowship with Jesus,
His coming is so near.
Come fellowship with Jesus,
Come now without delay.

He bids us watch, and work, and pray,
Our fellowship with Christ does pay.

This fellowship with Christ our Lord,
Brings grace and peace divine.
This fellowship so filled with joy,
Is vibrant and sublime.
Look up and shout with hope, and love,
And fellowship, from up above.

Restrained By Love

The plan of salvation
Agreed to by all
Father, Son, and Holy Spirit
All three restrained by Love.

Jesus lived a Holy life
Served mankind with compassion
Healed the sick, raised the dead
Yet they mocked and geared.

They stripped Him bare
They throned His head
They pierced His side
For them restrained by Love.

Their blinded eyes
Could not see the Love
Restraining Father, Son, and Holy Ghost
From their instant annihilation.

Humiliation endured by Jesus
Mockery scorn insults you bore
Warped perceptions clouded sinful minds
Let you drink the bitter cup.

No matter how terrible the ordeal
No matter how dreadful the suffering or bitter the cup.
Fulfillment of prophecy, completion of a promise
They were all restrained by Love.

Thank you Father for your mercy
Thank you Savior for your Love
Thank you Holy Spirit for your patience
It has moved and fashioned me.

Always, Anytime, and Whatever

*Bless the Lord **always**.*
His praise should always be in your heart.
He has been a faithful God,
To those who trust His Holy Word.

*Bless the Lord at **anytime**.*
Wherever you are, you should be ready.
Whenever it is, you should be prepared,
To adore Him, for He is a worthy God.

*Bless the Lord **wherever**.*
At home, in the car, at the mall
Any place is the best place,
For you to praise the Lord.

*Bless the Lord **whenever**.*
In the morning, at noon, in the midnight.
All the time is the right time,
For you to glorify the Lord.

*Bless the Lord **whatever**.*
No matter what the situation.
In spite of the condition or circumstance
Trust Him, adore Him, and magnify His Holy Name.

God Is Not Partial

God is not partial,
He created us all.
Without reservation, without favor,
He welcomes us short and tall.

Jews and Gentiles.
Black through White.
Give Him the honor due.
Do what is right and true.

God anointed Jesus,
With Holy Ghost Power.
He went about healing,
And setting captives free.

They put Him to death,
By nailing Him on a tree.
That was a great sacrifice.
For you and for me.

God is not partial.
He raised Him from the dead.
To represent everyone, everywhere
Who believe, receive, and care.
He is coming again,
For those who accept,
Pardon and forgiveness complete.
That are freely offered to all.

Extolling God is for everyone.
Giving His praise we all enjoy.
Worshipping Him is our delight.
He's God to each forever more.

What is Love

Love is Forgiving.
Love is Kind.
Love is Merciful.
Love is Sublime.
Love is Humble.
Love is a—glow.
Love has no stones to throw.

Love is Faithful.
Love is True.
Love is Thankful.
Love is Grand.
Love is Merciful.
Love is Gentle.
Love has no stones to throw.

Love is Peaceful.
Love is Patient.
Love is Honest.
Love is Gracious.
Love is Hopeful.
Love is Strong.
Love has no stones to throw

6

Kingdom Matters— Mercy & Grace

Pardon

Take away the filthy garments,
Off the representing believers.
Christ has taken the guilt of their sins
His robe of righteousness He gives.

Christ interposes when Satan seeks
To ruin the people of God
His human nature is linked with mankind
While His divine nature is one with God.

Let us, His people afflict our souls
Before Him.
Let us plead for purity of heart.
He will take away our filthy garments
Our inequity will pass away.

He clothes us with a change of raiment
And writes pardon against our names
Clothed in glorious apparel
Never to be defiled by corruption again.

Pardon it is
Pardon He gives
Pardon from sin and its shame
Guilty was I
Righteous is He
Thank You for pardoning me.

A Laodician Condition

You're neither hot nor cold
The condition of your life
Because your condition is unknown
I'll spew you out of my mouth!

You say you are rich and wealthy
You say you need nothing from me
But wretched you are, miserable, and naked
You're blind, poor, and destitute.

Receive your rebuke and be grateful
Be chastened, be zealous and repent
He's at the door and is knocking
For entrance, oh please let Him in.

The Laodician condition is not final
Just listen and open the door
Jesus is anxiously waiting
To help you to be either cold or hot.

Salt and light He command us,
To be in this world today
Don't lose your favor nor your light
They both are sure qualities of Him.

It's All About God As Creator

Satan was jealous that he could not create
So he bad mouth God to His creations
Some of them bought it and others did not
But he got many to question God intent.

God was so merciful, God was so great
He gave them time to change their thinking
But Satan had deceived them and blinded their eyes
To all of God's goodness and His creative powers.

Some came to their senses and returned to the throne.
As plea were sent forth for another chance.
Satan resisted along with his core
But others repented and were restored praise the Lord.

Satan got kicked out of heaven and home
He had a following for whom there was no room.
Only after they insisted to follow his lead
Into a pit of hell, doom, and misdeed.

Worship the Father, Son, and Holy Spirit.
Creatures created can't claim it as their own
They've never created or made to their glory.
A heaven, an earth and worth to begin with.

God is Creator, no other but He
Has all the power to save and make free
Let's give Him the glory, majesty, and praise
For all His goodness, for all of our days.

Send It Ahead

Send it ahead, send it ahead
Taking it with you is not in the plan
Send it ahead, send it ahead
That is holy, That is righteous, That is grand.

Send it ahead, send it ahead.
He'll send it to you if it'll go through you.
So that others can be blessed
And become part of His redemptive conquest.

Send it ahead, send it ahead.
And as you send it, it shall return,
In greater measure so shall it be
Send it ahead, send it with glee.

Send it ahead, send it ahead,
So that your stewardship be blessed of the Lord
Being a blessing to others, those who know Him not
Send it ahead, and defeat Satan's plot.

This is how treasurer is stored up in Heaven.
Protected by angels, accounted for by the Spirit
Secured by the Lord, assured by God.
Send it ahead, send it ahead.

Saving and Sustaining Grace

Grace has power to save
And Grace has power to sustain
Grace will save you
In the midst of the storm,
And sustain you till it's all over.

Thorn in the flesh so severe
Paul cried out to God for help
Begged as he prayed so fervently
But God said no my Son
The Grace that saved you will sustain you.

We to like Paul have thorns
We to experience your saving grace
How wonderful to know that
In all we think do or say,
Your grace that saves also sustains.

Your grace is sufficient
Because it saves and sustains
Your grace is sufficient
It's destine to prevail
No matter how the enemy assails.

Grace

We are saved by Grace.
We are kept and sustained by Grace.
Grace wakes you up in the morning
And goes with you all through the day.
Grace has a twin called Mercy
Who diagnosis the situation
But Grace fills the prescription.
Mercy finds you when you are lost
But it is Grace that takes you back home.
Grace serves your sin sick soul.
Grace shines in your darkest hour.
Grace holds you when the storm is raging.
Grace sees you when you're standing gazing.
Grace picks you up, turns you around.
Grace places your feet on solid ground.
Grace stands with you when friends forsake you.
Grace and Mercy will make you that Glory.
Grace and Mercy will make you shout Praise the Lord.
Grace and Mercy will make you shout Hallelujah.
Grace and Mercy will make you shout Amen.

Take Time

Take time to read the sacred Word.
Take time to understand.
That what it says comes from above,
From Him, to us with love.

Take time to pray and talk with God.
Take time to know His will.
Your will in His is all He asks.
For you He has the perfect tasks.

Take time to serve a soul in need.
Take time to lend a hand.
No one's an island to himself.
We're part of mission band.

Take time to walk and grow in grace.
Take time to apply His power.
The pardon that the Spirit brings.
Is real for every hour.

Take time to seek and find the lost.
Take time to tell His love.
This is our mission here below.
That's how He plans for us to grow.

Take time to ask for what you need,
Take time to let Him know
What He supplies will glorify,
His name, and cause will glow.

Take time to praise His Holy name,
Take time to lift Him high.
To Him whose love we all are drawn.
In prayer, and praise, our souls are born.

Nobody But You

You are the Almighty
You are the Exalted One
Powerful and all knowing
Gracious and forgiving
Nobody but You, Lord.

You are ever present
Always going where You're coming from
You are Covering and Shelter
For those who recognize the need
Nobody but You, Lord.

You are Reconciliation
You are Restoration
You are Willing and Able
Trustworthy and Dependable
Nobody but You, Lord.

Nobody can build a woman from a rib
Nobody can change a life from sinner to saint
Nobody can heal a broken heart and give sight to the blind
You are confident and assured
Nobody but You, Lord.

Nobody but You, Lord; Nobody but You.
Nobody but You, Lord, Nobody but You.

Nobody can calm the storms in the life
Nobody can speak to raging winds
Nobody can talk to the storm that rage
And get them to hush their fuss
Nobody but You, Lord.

He Went Back

Jesus the Savior can heal you.
He can also make you whole.
Just in an instant, I tell you
You can be made quite well.

Miracles of true healing
Come from above
For restoration and praise
From those who experience the joy.

Healing is an outcome job
Wholeness is from within
When grace and mercy are received
Thanksgiving and gratitude should be revealed.

Give Him Glory
Give Him Praise
Let them hear your voices raised
With Thanksgiving expressed to Him.

Return to the source of your healing
And receive wholeness for God as well.
Thanksgiving and gratitude are expressions
of a grateful Spirit from the heart.

Receive what others don't get
When Thanksgiving and praise are not expressed
The avenue for wholeness from Jesus
Is adoration, honor, worship and awe.

Return and express that to your healer
And leave rejoicing as well.
He can do much more than heal you.
He will make you whole as well.

Give Him Glory
Give Him Praise
Let Him hear your voices raised
With sounds of Thanksgiving to Him.

Thanksgiving and Praise

Jesus the Savior can heal.
He can also make you whole.
But just in an instant,
You can be made well.

Miracles of healing,
Come from above.
For restoration and praise.
From those who receive

Healing is an outside job.
Wholeness is from within.
When grace and mercy are received.
Thanksgiving and gratitude must be revealed.

Give Him glory
Give Him praise
Let them hear your voices raised
With Thanksgiving expressed from within

Return to the source of your healing,
And receive wholeness as well.
Thanksgiving and praise in gratitude,
Is the avenue for wholeness from Christ.

Receive what others don't get.
When Thanksgiving is not expressed,
But return and say to your healer,
And rejoice for wellness and wholeness.

Wholeness and wellness,
Are blessings we know.
Praise and Thanksgiving,
Are responses from within.

Give Him Thanksgiving
Give Him praise
Always express your gratitude
Get more wellness be whole.

At the Throne and Not the Cross

At the Throne and not the Cross,
Is where the action is today.
At the Throne, at the Throne,
He bids us to come to find the way.

At the Throne his mercy is dispersed.
At the Throne He also gives us grace.
He invites us come with the bold confidence.
There is no other way, there is no other place.

With full assurance, and with guarantee,
He listens, pardons, and forgives.
Deliverance and compassion come, freely from His Throne.
His divine energy is given to make us whole.

It's not at the cross or at Bethlehem.
Mt. Sinai, Golgotha or at the tomb.
Jerusalem no, it's at the Throne
Where the action is full bloom.

At the Throne, not the cross,
The light of God is clearly seen.
There we go meet our need
That's where the action is supreme.

At the Throne is God the Father.
At the Throne is God the Son.
At the Throne is God the Holy Spirit.
One in three, and three in one.

He's Worthy Give Him Praise

He's worthy to be praised.
He's worthy to be praised.
He's worthy to be praised.
His name we do adore.

He's worthy of thanksgiving.
He's worthy of thanksgiving.
He's worthy of thanksgiving.
His name we glorify.

He's worthy of all honor.
He's worthy of all honor.
He's worthy of all honor.
His name we magnify.

We adore you, we glorify you.
We magnify you, you're God and Lord of all.
We adore Him, We glorify Him.
We magnify Him, He's God and Lord of all.

Praise The Lord

Praise the Lord for who He Is.
Praise the Lord for what He's Done.
Praise the Lord for what He Gives.
Praise, Praise, Praise Ye the Lord.

Praise the Lord for Love so Safe.
Praise the Lord for a hiding Place.
Praise the Lord for bringing you Through.
Praise, Praise, Praise Ye the Lord.

Praise the Lord for Mercy and Faith.
Praise the Lord for Victory in This Race.
Praise the Lord for Strength and Power.
Praise, Praise, Praise Ye the Lord.

Praise the Lord for Taking Our Place.
Praise the Lord for His Saving Grace.
Praise the Lord for Promises so grand.
Praise, Praise, Praise Ye the Lord.

Praise God to Whom All Praise is Due.
Praise God who has Your Plan in View.
Praise Him in the Morning, Praise Him at Night.
Praise God for His Magnificent Light.

Magnify Him

Oh magnify the Lord with me
Make His name known
Oh glorify the Lord with me
Let His power be seen.

Oh magnify the Lord with me
His majesty so grand
All the earth must give Him honor
He's worthy, He's holy, He stands alone.

Oh magnify the Lord with me
Tell His wondrous plan
Offering freedom and salvation
To all who sense the need.

Jesus Christ His Holy Son
Came to die for everyone
Magnify Him, glorify Him
God, Creator, Father, Friend.

Here is how we magnify Him
In our lives and in our plans
Let the Holy Spirit come within us
Give Him authority to have His way.

Praise and Thanksgiving always follows
When we make Him Lord of all
Thank you Father for Your Power
For your majesty and might.

The Wills of God

God created Man to praise and worship
In the presence of his Maker
This life to live forever more
Was God's Intentional Will.

Sin interrupted God's Intentional Will
The enemy thought he'd won
But God the Father, God the Son
And God the Holy Spirit
Put in place God's circumstantial will.

The grace of God, the mercy of the Father
And God's forgiving love
Nullifies and cushions the blows of the enemy
And activates God's ultimate will.

We thank you God for your Wills
Intentional, Circumstantial, and Ultimate
Keep us by your grace and mercy
Include us within your perfect Will

When You Are Converted

Nicodemus was a good man,
But he was not converted.
So Jesus met with him at night,
And told him conversion was a must.

Peter was a good man,
But he too was not converted.
And Jesus said to him,
When you are converted, teach.

Membership is admirable,
But discipling is the thing.
Accepting Jesus as Savior,
Begins your journey home.

Come let's walk with Jesus
By the Spirit's power.
Now that you're converted,
It's every moment, every hour.

When you are converted,
You'll be spiritually committed.
When you are converted,
You're heart and soul submitted.

Worthy to be Worshipped and Praised

Magnificent Father
Holy God
Gracious Creator,
Worshipful Lord.
Worthy to be worshipped.
Worthy to be praised.

Loving Savior,
Merciful Provider.
Amazing Redeemer,
Blessed is Your Name.
Worthy to be worshipped
Worthy to be praised.

Mediator Advocate,
Prince of Peace.
Deliverer Protector
Conquering King
Worthy to be worshipped
Worthy to be praised.

Faithful and true,
None other like You.
Glorious is Your goodness,
Shown radiantly in Him.
Offering redemption,
Restoring Your Image.
Worthy to be worshipped
Worthy to be praised.

When We Sing The Word

The Word is powerful and mighty,
When we hide it in our hearts.
Many could be singing loud,
But it might not be the word.

It has of cause entertaining value,
But we sing to praise the Lord,
When we sing the Word,
Yes when we sing the Word.

When we sing the Word,
It celebrates our God,
It teaches about God,
It exalts the only God,
It extols and magnifies God,
When we sing the Word.

When we sing the Word,
It invites us to commune with God,
It proclaims the goodness and mercy of God,
It gives praise to the one and only God,
It shows that He's worthy to be praised,
When we sing the Word.

When we sing the Word,
It motivates and challenges concentration,
It prepares us to hear the spoken Word,
It calls us to fellowship with each other,
It helps us to honor and glorify His Name,
When we sing the Word.

When we sing the Word,
It brings God's presence into our midst,
It invites our dedication and commitment,
It evokes sacrifice and thanksgiving,
It ignites devotion and dedication.
Be blessed by the best, and sing the Word.

7

Prayer—Peace—Persistence—Pardon—Forgiveness

Holy Spirit

Holy Spirit, Counselor, and Friend.
Holy Spirit, Comforter Grand.
Holy Spirit mighty in Power.
Fill me, control me, this very hour.

Keep my feet in the path to stay
Give me power, mercy, and grace
Speak the truth through me each day
Give it direction and purpose I pray.

Give me favor with God and man.
Let them see in me His mighty plan.
Do your work within my life,
Keep me yielded, humble, and contrite.

Holy Spirit, guardian friend
Holy Spirit here, hold my hand
Holy Spirit peaceful and strong
Fill me, Keep me, guide me to the end.

Lord Teach Us How to Pray

We know not how to pray aright
No one has taught us how
You used it for Your every need
Lord teach us, Lord, show us how.

We sing, we pray and worship you
And feel your presence near
But oh what joy with open hearts
We speak to You in prayer.

Of all the things You've done for us
We thank you most for Your sacrifice
For health and strength and love so dear
We thank You for a listening ear.

We promise Lord to talk with You,
From time to time each day
We hope to talk in simple faith,
What privilege, what pleasure, what grace.

I Want To Know You

I'm acquainted with what You have done.
I'm acquainted with who You are.
I'm acquainted with how You act.
But, I want to know You, Lord.

I understand how You parted the sea.
I understand how You raised the dead.
I understand how You walk on water.
But I want to know You, Lord.

I see the birds flying by Your power.
I see the fish swing every hour.
I see the clouds and the stars and skies.
But I want to know You, Lord.

I feel Your presence in my space.
I feel Your love and Your grace.
I feel compassion, care, and power.
But I want to know You, Lord.

I know Your presence will go with me.
I know Your favor has followed me.
I know Your name—I am that I am.
But I want to know You, Lord.

I want to find favor in Your sight, Lord.
I want to be acquainted with You, Lord.
I also want to understand You, Lord.
But most of all, I want to know You, Lord.

Whatever You're Doing Lord

Whatever You're doing to save souls-
Preaching the gospel
Feeding the hungry
Clothing the naked
Setting sin's captives free
Lord, please, don't do it without us.

Whatever You're doing to warn the world
Allowing tragedies and disasters
Permitting destruction and devastation
Releasing signs and wonders in diverse places
Fulfilling prophecy in our present time
Please, Lord, don't do it without us.

Whatever You're doing in these last days
Healing the sick
Raising the dead
Making the dumb to talk
Causing the lame to walk
Please, Lord, don't do it without me.

Whatever You're doing before probation closes
Infusing strength to the weary
Giving hope to the hopeless
Helping the unbeliever
Restoring the sight to the blind
Lord, please, don't do it without me.

Whatever You're doing to hasten Your return
Giving boldness to delivery of the Word
Acceptance to those who are received
Creating urgency to our commission
Discipleship to our membership efforts
Lord, please don't do it without me.

Whatever You're doing Lord, please do it, but
Don't do it without me.
Whatever You're doing Lord, please do it, but
Don't do it without us.

God Shuts The Door

The opened door we all expect
But one day it will be shut.
Warnings came and for a moment
We took notice
And one day the door was no longer opened.

Who shut the door we asked around.
Was it God or our very choices.
We heard the claims and saw the signs.
Never thought the time was over.

It's time to end the controversy
Between evil and good God said
Let's call it quits and completely done
The time has come to shut the door.

They will come knocking I am sure
But too late twill be the cry
To enter the Ark of Safety and Peace
God has the key and all opportunities cease

The door is shut
The door is shut
Thank God I'm in and not out
My sins forgiven
My name retained
Oh praise the Lord
His name proclaim.

Pushing Against The Pillows

Sin will not be overlooked.
Sin must be overcome.
Sin will be excluded when confessed
And forsaken.
When we push against the Pillows.

Only the pure in heart will enter Heaven.
You just cannot bluff your way in.
Ask for strength in the battle,
And keep pushing against the Pillows.

Only hearts that are loyal will enter
Fully surrendered to the Savior and Lord.
You just cannot con your way in.
Keep on pushing against the Pillows.

There must be an examination and investigation,
Of every candidate for external redemption.
You just can't jive your way in.
You have to push against the Pillows.

It must be determined,
Whether the candidate is sufficiently rehabilitated.
Before being released into a Heavenly atmosphere,
As she/he pushes against the Pillows.

Well done will be the declaration
When the Pillows of sin are brought down
Your roots were never destroyed
Your hair began to grow as you pushed against the Pillows.

Keep pushing against the Pillows.
Your reward is eternal life with the Savior.
Keep pushing and praising the Creator, Redeemer.
Your victorious pushing has eternal reward.

Hear Me Lord

Hear me Lord and Savior,
And Hearken to my plea.
Give me some attention,
And my fears will flee.

Nothing else will comfort,
My soul's desire just now.
Let me know you hear me,
In my darkest hour.

Keep me safe from danger,
Seen and those unseen.
Bless me with discernment.
Make me fit and clean.

Thank you Lord for hearing,
My plea, my call today.
Always be here beside me.
Father, God I pray.

It Was Mary

It was Mary of Magdale
The sister if Martha
It was Mary, the woman
Thrown down at His feet
It was Mary, Lazarus sister
Who was at the Tomb
That early Sunday Morning.

It was Mary whose demons
Were expelled by the Master
It was Mary who was first to tell the news
Of an unsealed tomb and an empty grove
It was Mary who stayed
After Peter and John left
Who encountered two angels who gave her the good news.

It was beloved Mary
Who blinded with tears
Saw the form of a man she thought was the gardener
But the gentle voice she heard
Which she had heard before
Was caring asking why for the tears
Sir, she pleaded pleas tell where you've laid Him.

It was Mary who said
I'll take Him away
Mary, the voice called and recognizing the voice
She moved to embrace her Lord
Not at this time the Savior said
I must quickly ascend to the Father
And Mary was pleased to see Him alive.

Do me a favor the Master asked
Go tell My disciples that I am alive
Tell them the good news of resurrection
Many complied with her Lord's request
It was Mary who first preached the resurrection
Why was she entrusted to tell the good news
He knew she'd be faithful and true.

It was Mary who set at the feet of Jesus
It was Mary who sought to know more about Him
It was Mary who poured upon His head the precious anointing oil
It was Mary who bathed His feet with her tears
It was Mary who stood beside the old rugged cross
It was Mary who followed Him
She was the first at the tomb and the first to proclaim a risen
Savior.

8

Redemption—Restoration— Reconcilization

It's Not A Matter

It's not a matter of where you live,
but how you live where you live.

It's not a matter of who you are,
but what you do with who you are.

It's not a matter of when you start,
but where you're headed when you start.

It's not a matter of what you're doing,
but how you're doing what you're doing.

It's not a matter of what you say,
but how you say what you say.

It's not a matter of what you see,
but how you view what you see.

It's not a matter of what you hear,
but what you think about what you hear.

It's not a matter of what you know,
but what you do with what you know.

It's not a matter of how you look,
but how you feel about how you look.

It's not a matter of how you walk,
but where you go when you walk.

Where Goest Thou

Where goest thou,
The fight has just begun.
When goest thou,
Don't leave before the victory's won.
Come fight and fight and struggle on,
Don't let the Captain come and find you gone.

Where goest thou,
Satan's power is all around.
Where goest thou,
No safe shelter out there can be found.
Those outside are trying to come in,
Let's stick to the task and rescue all we can win.

Where goest thou,
When Jesus will soon come.
Where goest thou,
There's much work to be done.
Workers why wait till it's but the last hour,
Fight on in our labor with might and power.

Where goest thou,
The end is in sight.
Walk in His way,
Do not, go astray.
Keeping His word in obedience and faith,
Jesus is coming, Let us watch, let us wait.

Saved By Grace But Judged By Works

I am so glad to be saved by grace
The precious blood of Christ was shed
God the Father gave His all for me
I'm so glad that I'm saved by grace.

He gives me power to live for Him
My armor's on to fight to win
New mercies gained from day to day
Because I'm saved by grace.

He pardons me of all my sins
And bids me to go on
I'm moving up from strength to strength
Compliments of His saving grace.

I'll stay obedient to His word
My Armor's on, all parts in place
His Spirit guide along the way
Thank God for mercy and His grace.

I'm saved by grace
His blood was shed
God gave His all for me
My gratitude, obedience shows
I know I'm saved by grace.

The Anointing

The anointing is for service
The anointing is being empowered
To set captives free, unshackles jokes
And minister to the poor.

To anoint is the gift of authority
To walk in righteousness
Character sustains the anointing
And assures the presence of God.

The anointing will remove burdens
Through the manifestation of the Lord
We have to walk in faith and trust
He's with us all the way.

Don't Let Go Too Soon

Do not let go no matter what,
The plight might look or be
Do not let go hold on with might
Victory is just in sight.

Do not let go persist at will.
Determined as never before
To fight to the end in every case
Make prayer and praise your spiritual base.

Do not let go help is on the way
From heaven the source of your strength
Testing your resolve to hold on
To promises made to you.

I'll never leave you, nor forsake
Is my Word in your fight
Faithful am I to my Word
To you my child, well done.

Reclaiming Those Who Left

Somehow they left without notice
I did not say my goodbye
So let me determine to reach them
And invite them of come back home.

There's nothing out there to protect them
From Satan and his destructive snares
Oh God make us the kind of people
To celebrate their return to the fold.

The environment We create in fellowship
From week to week let it be
The kind that will speak to their value
To you and as well to us.

Bring us together dear Father
Once again in thy name to praise
Father, Son, and the Spirit
To Thee Thanksgiving is raised.

The Repentant Sinner

Sin is sin, no matter what
Great or small, little or big
No one is exempt
No one is excused.

Confession is the sinner's out
A mechanism safe and sure
Repentance from the heart assures
God's grace is what you need.

Against God the sin is done
No matter who's involved
The death of Christ for every sin
Brings victory without, within.

Forgiveness makes you right
Restoration puts you on track again
Cleansing comes from God above,
Grace and Mercy will keep you there.

When Quit Looks Good

I'm not one for complaining
In times good or bad
But I can say right up front
When quit looks good.

Complaining makes no difference
The matter seems to persist
That is just the very time
When quit looks real good.

Quit looks good,
When you're feeling bad
Quit looks good when you're sad within
Quit looks good,
When your efforts fail
Quit looks good,
When your enemies prevail.

But to quit is not in my DNA
No matter how bleak and drear
Something within controls my will
No quitting, not now, not ever.

9

Salvation—Thanksgiving—Trust—Worship

To His Glory

God give us a will, but we have to work it.
God gives us a promise, but we have to claim it.
God gives us the Word, but we have to obey it.
God gives us purpose, but we have to comply with it.
God gives us talent, but we have to exhibit it.
God gives us Spiritual gifts, but we have to use them.

To His Glory
To His Honor
To His Praise

Salvation is made possible, but we have to declare it.
Redemption is available, but we have to know it.
Reformation is ours, but we have to wear it.
Restoration is ours, but we have to embrace it.
Justification is ours, but we have to accept it.
Sanctification is ours, but we have to show it.

To His Glory
To His Honor
To His Praise

Grace is mine but I have to proclaim it.
Mercy is mine, but I have to trust it.
Favor is mine, but I have to announce it.
Protection is mine, but I have to see it.
Holiness is mine, but I have to wear it.

Victory is mine, but I have to shout it.

To His Glory
To His Honor
To His Praise

Men of Valor

Men of God, firmly stand.
On His Word, embrace His plan.
In our finding, give him praise.
For our well-being and numbered days.

Men of vision, and of might.
God will lead us by His light.
From His word, just use His lamp.
He has provided for His camp.

Men of character, full of faith.
Reaching out to others before it's too late.
Given to fellowship, friendship delight.
Come on to this journey, We're preparing for flight.

Men of distinction, grace and valor
Representing Jesus in all that we do.
Looking to the Savior, Lord of our life.
He'll draw them to us whomever He might.

Give Him glory, give His praise.
Let Him hear your voices raise.
Thanksgiving is in order, He's worthy we know.
In gratitude to serve Him, His blessings we'll show.

God Is Still Coming

He came to earth to rescue us
From sin, and, shame, and death
His love found us without a plan
To overcome the enemy's threat.

My rescue plan is sound and good
But you have a role to play
No more can you sit idly by
And let your soul waste away.

Jesus went looking for the demonic
Occupied by legions of demons galore
He spoke to the occupants of his soul
And they fled to bother Him no more.

The mission is over once contact is made
The demons know Him by name
Jesus our Wonderful Savior and Lord
Come through to deliver and heal.

Jesus is still coming we know
To demonstrate His love for us all
In spite of the acts of the devil
His every distraction to impede.

The Warfare Is Over Worship

Worship causes us to focus on God.
The Devil does not want us to do this.
Worship pays tribute to God.
The Devil does not want us to do this.

Worship allows us to glorify God.
The Devil does not want us to do this.
Worship takes our thoughts away from our
Problems and places them on God.
The Devil does not want us to do this.

Worship builds our confidence in God.
The Devil does not want us to do this.
Worship gives us an opportunity to have
God intervene in our lives and situations.
The Devil does not want us to do this.

Worship keeps our relationship fresh with God.
The Devil does not want us to do this.
Worship helps us to establish unity with
Sons and daughters of God.
The Devil does not want us to do this.

It is evident that the Devil is an enemy of our souls, and
Does not want us to receive the blessings of
God which come from a relationship with the Lord
Through worship and praise.

A Wonderful God

You're merciful and gracious.
Slow to be angry forever.
Does not punish us according to our sins.
Show mercy to those who fear.

You're a Father who pities your children.
When in sin they discover themselves.
Helpless as if there's no helper.
Strength to deliver their soul.

Oh what a wonderful father.
Who refuses to reject us outright.
Nor treat us according to our transgressions.
We willfully and deliberately display.

Come to our rescue dear Saviour.
Our inequities and sins are so great.
Cast them away from your presence.
And give us peace within we pray.

Repent For Deliverance

Turn yourself to me.
Have mercy on my condition
I am desolate and afflicted
I need help for my situation.

The troubles of my heart
Have enlarged and out of control
Oh bring me out of my distress
Be the balm and healer of my soul.

Look on my affliction,
My pain and sorrow
Forgive all my sins and inequities
Your grace and your mercy restore.

Thank you for your forgiveness
So kind compassionate is He
He's the joy of my salvation
Praise God He delivered me

Obedience to God is Not Optional

Obedience is not optional
To the God of the Universe
Any expression of the Gospel
Must result in complete obedience.

We are called to obedience
Any expression to the contrary
God takes this matter seriously
To do otherwise is a false response.

Obedience to the Word
Is essential to salvation
God knows your heart
Your will, you have control.

Give Him obedience based on love
Let gratitude fill your heart
Where grace has been given
Loyalty and adherence should be evident.

God Starts It

He started it
I can't tell when
I felt the change within
But now I'm sure
It was from Him
I feel so free from sin.

A good thing God will start in you
To give purpose, direction, and hope
Remember now who made the move
Remember whose in control.

His move SAYS He's committed
To whatever good was started
Trust in His word and in His love
He'll safely move you along.

Completion is His final goal
His work in us complete
When Jesus comes to take us home
In heaven to live with Him.

Thanksgiving

Thanksgiving is for grateful hearts
To praise and thank the Lord
Thank Him for His goodness
Thank Him for being faithful.

Thanksgiving is for those who care
And those whose hopes are high
Thanksgiving does what nothing else
Can do to make you whole.

Thanksgiving is an inside job
Welding up within the heart
To be expressed for all to hear
And for all who say they care.

Give thanks to God in all His ways
Father, Son, and Holy Ghost
No other act of gratitude
Should express our love and worth.

10

Warning—Sacrifice—Love—
The Church

Vindication

Satan has made bold accusations,
All around the throne of God.
Angels, listened and they wandered,
As he spread his vicious lies.

God the Father flexed His patience,
In the courts of heaven above.
Here you have a being created,
Talking ill about a God of Love.

Lines were drawn, positions taken.
Satan took his case to all.
Father, Son, and Holy Spirit,
Watched as Angels took His side.

War was started up in Heaven.
Satan lost and got thrown out.
On to Earth he used deception
To control both Earth and man.

It was for this that Jesus died.
To vindicate His Father's name.
When we accept His sacrifice and mercy,
We too become vindicators of His name.

As believers for whom Jesus died
Vindication is what He ask of us.
What a task, a privilege and an honor
To show the universe that Satan lied.

It was for both the Savior died
His Father's character, and my soul to glorify
Let's join with Angels who rewarded faithful
To celebrate and lift Him high.
Vindication, Vindication, Vindication of our God.

He Sacrificed His Life

He bled and died,
For you and for me.
Nothing else would satisfy,
But Jesus precious blood.

Blood of Salvation.
Blood of Redemption.
God sent Himself to die,
And came in the person of His Son.

Oh, what a sacrifice.
Oh, what great love.
Shedding His precious blood.
For us we'll forever adore.

Life indeed is in the blood.
Shed from the foundation of the World.
That powerful blood is a cleaning stream,
Reaching deep down into the depths of our best.

The strength of the blood,
Was never questioned.
Because of the work it does in the life.
It's power and effect are forever sure.

We are to save the lost at any cost.
We are to teach the saved to serve.
Inside the church as well as outside.
God's grace will save and sustain.

It was for both the Savior died
His Father's character, and my soul to glorify
Let's join with Angels who rewarded faithful
To celebrate and lift Him high.
Vindication, Vindication, Vindication of our God.

The Power of the Blood

Our redemption is in Jesus.
His blood blots out every sin.
The blood is a symbol of our Salvation
And brings us peace from within.

The blood brings our remission
For there's no forgiveness without it.
The blood affects justification,
And gives us right standing with God.

Restoration is affected by the blood.
So when the blood is safely applied,
Your justification is assured by Him.
Our names are retained, our sins blotted out.

The blood is a cleansing agent.
It washes sin and dirt away.
The power and value of the blood,
Gives hope and joy to stay.

The blood brings access to the Throne,
For everything we need from God.
Power, strength, and faith to overcome sin,
The snares and traps of the enemy.

Go on and get washed in the blood my friend.
Make sure you are clean within.
Washed in the blood by Christ above.
The invitation is opened, to all, go in.

Love Me

Love Me and let me cover you.
Love Me and be made clean.
Love Me and have your sins forgiven.
Love Me and I'll intervene.

My love came looking for you,
To take your sins away.
My love will bring reconcilization.
My love will make you whole.

Love Me and you will love yourself.
Love Me and you'll love others.
Even your enemies and your foes.
Love Me and they will know.

My love will give you restoration.
Your joy will be brand new.
Transgressions will be forgiven.
Inequities will be covered too.

Love Me and receive mercy.
Love Me and get loving kindness.
Love me with all your strength.
Love me with all your might.

My love will rescue from despair,
From destruction and doom.
Complete and full receive it now.
My love is all you need.

Rejoice because My love is pure.
No doubt, no fear, no scorn.
My love is sure and guaranteed
From now throughout eternity.

I Press On

I Press on with persistence and power.
I Press on, but counting the cost.
I Press on with God as my leader.
I Press on in Jesus' Name.

I Press on no matter what the problem.
I Press on no matter the care.
I have direction from God the Father.
Written clearly in His Word.

I Press onward and also upward.
Cares all gone, and problem free.
Pressing with courage with released blessing.
Jesus my Savior has delivered me.

Now that He's given His Holy Spirit.
Freedom, deliverance so joyfully.
My sights are heaven bound.
I'm safe and secure, don't you see.
I will Press on
Let us Press On.

Be Content

I have the victory being content,
No matter what the state I'm in.
Whether living humbly or whether in plenty
I'm satisfied, not disgusted, nor disturbed.

God has seasons already planned.
All circumstances under control.
In different circumstances or those contained.
No expression of discontent on my face.

I'm gratified to experience promised abundance.
But that for a while, I'm not sure.
Don't have to last in this wicked world
Where time and seasons constantly change.

Lord teach us to free all life challenges.
Whether in much or in less.
Joyful and pleased with what You have done.
And what You are planning to do.

You are our sufficiency.
We you're children finally believe.
Whether in drought or prosperity.
Teach us Your will as revealed.

Standing Alone In Character

Character is built persistently
It is done with intent
Ups and downs are all designed
To test our resolve.

Character is built in overcoming
Trials and temptation will come
Divine input given through sanctification
Prayrd for and received.

Character is built in obedience
To instructions and commands of God
We are on trial for heaven
To live with the Lord forever more.

Character is built in surrender
Thy will not mine be done
Behold I'm coming quickly
Rewards I'll have for everyone.

When we stand alone in character
Successful and victorious we'll be
Overcoming all of Satan's temptations
Obedience to God is the key.

The Tomb Was Empty

His death was sad to those
Who cared and wished Him well
The tomb was empty when they got there
He rose just as He said.

Fear swept through the hearts of those
Who loved and cherished Him
And Angel came to comfort them
To restore peace and good will.

They needed to be enlightened
About the reality of His resurrection
When spiritual invade the safety of our world
God understands and intervenes.

And so it is with some and many
When troubled by spiritual events
Dramatic and even miraculous demonstrations
Will empty every Tomb to truth.

God delights and appreciates
The impact of spiritual light
Brightly shining in places of darkness
The greatest of all is that the Tomb is empty.

Keep Yourselves
"In the Love of God"

Keep yourself in the Love of God.
In the Love of God you're safe.
His Love is sure, His Love is great.
It's faithful, it's satisfying, it's safe.

Keep yourself in the Love of God.
Follow after Godly things.
His word is your guide in every case.
Hold on, move on, in faith.

Keep yourself in the Love of God.
Receive His mercies and grace.
He'll snatch you from your fears and doubts.
He has promised life eternal.

Keep yourself in the Love of God.
He is able to keep you from stumbling.
You'll stand in God's presence without blame
And live with the Saints forever.

That They May Be One

As Your Father, are in Me
And I, Father in You
Make them Holy Father
May they be one in us.

So the World may know
That I was sent by Thee
And the Holy Spirit
Sent to them through Me.

Give them grace to follow
All they know of Thee
Everything I've taught them
Make them a willing lot for Me.

We Are The Church

We are the church
We are God's children
We are the ones
To show a better way
Through our own living
There's a choice we're making
Denying our own lives
It's true, we show a better way
Through Jesus Christ!

We are the church
We are God's people
We are the ones
To take His word
To every creature
In His time He's coming
To make His claim on us
We must be ready to welcome Him
When He returns.

We are the church
We are God's witness
We are the ones to live a Holy life
Through righteous living
There's a day a coming
When all things shall be known
So let us live a better life
In Jesus name.

11

Service—Reward—Mission— Assignment—Baptism— Holy Spirit

His Call To Serve

God called Moses on a Deliverance Mission
Moses confessed that he had a problem
Not with the mission, but with the call
I can't talk he said, call someone else.

No, said the Lord, this is your call
Don't be concerned about you impediment
My words will be yours in every case
The mission is not yours, it is mine.

So go your way,
I'll speak through you
And watch what happens next
Your victories will come through me
Don't fear, don't sweat, don't fret.

Thank you Lord for your call,
To action every day of my life
There is no greater joy to work with You
And see your plans fulfilled.

I Never Knew You

Rejection from anyone in any form,
Is difficult to accept.
It causes pain inside and out.
You sit and wonder why.

It is especially hard to hear one say.
I never knew you to be.
A friend, a son, or daughter.
It's hard to be set aside.

But when it comes from one who knows,
The when, the why, the where.
It dulls the mind, freezes the soul.
And clouds your heart in fear.

King Jesus knows before He makes,
Those solemn words to hear.
He sees your heart, behavior to
And declares, I never knew.

Before He says those words to you,
Give Him your mind, your soul.
Your heart is also what he wants.
Those words you'll never hear.

Stewards of God

What an honor, what a privilege
Bestowed by a loving and caring God
To be stewards of possessions and His Grace
He's the owner of all things
Creator, Proprietor, and Manager.

Money, houses, and land
Garments, furniture, and luxuries
Do not belong to us
We are pilgrims, we are strangers
All is from God as a trust
Sumptuous living is not a most
Nor the intent when trusted with much.

Our temporal blessings are given in trust
To determine our take of eternal riches
Let us endure the proving of God
So that we may receive that purchased possession
Glory, and honor, and immortality.

We have to recognize God's ownership
In how we manage what is entrusted
Remember how He can take you and leave the stuff
He can take the stuff and leave you
He can also take you and your stuff.

We are granted what we need
For health and life even in abundance
We are supplied from God
With talents and the like
and placed in the word
To do a work appointed by Him.

The Truth Takes Hold

Take hold of the truth
And let it take hold of you
The truth in us and we in the truth
The truth we hold is from Heaven.

The truth accomplishes for us
What nothing else can do
It sanctifies and gives us moral fitness
The truth we hold is from above.

The truth must find a place inside
To commence it purifying work
Refining, defining the path to take
The truth we hold has heavenly origin.

It makes us kind, pure, and clean
It elevates the mind and soul
It rids of pride and selfishness
The truth we hold is God's.

I am the truth to you I come
To set you free from sin
Embrace the truth it free to all
Jesus invites you to.

Baptize and Fill Me

Baptize me Lord,
With the gift of the Holy Spirit.
Fill me with His power,
T o live and glorify (You) Thee.

Fill me with your Spirit,
For the journey Lord.
His need is for every hour.
With Him every day's a joy.

The gift of the Holy Spirit,
Is given to those in need.
The assurance of a Savior,
Who died from Sin to Save.

The filling of the Holy Spirit,
Will give you power within.
To live and give God glory,
For the victory He brings.

Execute the Vision

Write the vision
Make it clear
Confirm the vision
Execute the vision
Move comfortably
Move swiftly
Move diligently
Move without hesitation
People will perish
Without a vision
That is what the Bible says
But it must be written
Plainly and clearly
Implemented by those who see
There is no exception
To the vision rule
With a clear understanding
Of God's given mission
Assigned to His children
Here to this earth
We stay closely connected
To the vision Giver
Great exploits can be accomplished
For the Kingdom of God

Heavenly Dove

Heavenly Dove
Faithful Guide
Great is your presence
Living Inside
Comforting Influence
Glory Hallelujah
Leading me to worship
Leading me to praise.

Worthy to be worshipped
Worthy to be praised
Father, Son, and Holy Spirit,
One in all, and
All in one
Creator, Sustainer,
Comforter Friend
Worthy to be worshipped
Worthy to be praised.

His Reward

When He shall come with His reward
A reflection of His character my life must be
His character reflector my life must be
No other way I'll see His face
In peace and in harmony.

That day two groups will be revealed
The good to life eternal
The bad to death complete
The saints shall reign and gain eternity
With Him for all eternity.

My hope is to be prepared for Him,
Whenever He says it's done
Righteous still, Holy still
Up we'll go, Resurrected, Claimed, Delivered.

His reward, my reward
To share eternity with Thee
When He comes, when He comes
His reward, come be with me.

Serve The Lord

Serve the Lord with gladness
Not madness nor with sadness
Serve the Lord with boldness
Give Him honor, give Him praise.

Serve the Lord in singing
Keep praises on your lips
Serve the Lord with Thanksgiving
Let praises fill your heart.

Serve Him for His goodness
His faithfulness is sure
Serve Him for anointing
Your walk with acts of love.

Serve the Lord with boldness
The anointing is on your life
To teach, to preach, to testify
Of His goodness, kindness, and love.

Serve the Lord in gratitude
For love, for peace, and forgiveness
Where grace has been received
Gratitude should be revealed.

So, Be

We are called to serve
Utilizing whatever gifts,
Have been placed in our hands.
So, Be.
Be blessed to be a blessing
Be faithful to the dreams or visions
God has birth in you.
Be faithful to your God—given purpose and assignment.
God becomes responsible for ultimate success.
Be the best you can with what you have,
And if you do that, God will do the rest.
Be grateful for what the Lord has done,
Is doing and will do.
Be a beacon of hope and opportunity.
Be a winner and don't quit, for quitters never win.
Be a possibility through Christ.
Be encouraged and an Encourager.

Be a redemptive change agent.
Be a model of Jesus, modeling the
Principles of Christian love on everyday living.
Be a witness to the goodness, grace, and mercies of God.
Be a leader, and a follower, in authority and under authority.
Be an example of spiritual growth and development.
Be obedient and trust in the Lord.
Be a servant of God to the people.
Be passionate in pursuit of God and holiness.
Be salt and be light.
Be a winner and not a loser.
Be strong in the Lord and in the
Power of His might (Ephesians 6:10)
Be whatever God calls you to be.
Just Be.

Well Done

To many He'll say well done
You did your part for Me
To others He'll say depart
You acted none too smart.

What will it be that hit your ears
When Jesus shall appear
What have you done as He command
Go tell some souls I've come.

Well Done is said to those who heed
The commission that Jesus gave
To go into the highways
To introduce them to Him.

Go tell the wondrous story
That Jesus came down from glory
To make you well and Holy
To reign and dwell with Him.

Well done rewards surrender.
Well done rewards obedience.
Well done rewards commitment.
Well done rewards persistence.

Welcome home my children
Sit down and please rejoice
You have been so victorious
Saved now and free from sin

Would you hear the well done
From the Savior's lips
When He comes from glory
To end Satan's reign of sin.

We'll Get There

He did His work on Earth.
He lived, He died, He arose.
He left to give assurance
That one day we'll get there.

He promised to share forever
With those who do His will
His advocacy before the throne
Is to make certain we'll get there.

He promised to share forever
With those who do His will
His advocacy before the throne
Is to make certain that we'll get there.

He left His Word
A map to guide our way
The Holy Spirit continues His work
To the end that we'll get there.

He stands before the Father
With reunion on His mind
His mediation on our behalf
Guarantees that we'll get there.

We'll get there
We'll get there
The faith of all the ages
We'll get there
His promises are in the Word
We'll get there
We'll get there
The blessed hope of all.